NATURAL DISASTERS

by Mary Meinking

Cody Koala

An Imprint of Pop!

popbooksonline.com

abdopublishing.com

Published by Pop!, a division of ABDO, PO Box 398166, Minneapolis, Minnesota 55439. Copyright © 2019 by POP, LLC. International copyrights reserved in all countries. No part of this book may be reproduced in any form without written permission from the publisher. Pop!™ is a trademark and logo of POP, LLC.

Printed in the United States of America, North Mankato, Minnesota

042018
092018

Cover Photo: Shutterstock Images
Interior Photos: Shutterstock Images, 1, 7 (top), 19, 20; iStockphoto, 5, 7 (bottom left), 8, 11, 13, 14, 16

Editor: Meg Gaertner
Series Designer: Laura Mitchell

Library of Congress Control Number: 2017963478
Publisher's Cataloging-in-Publication Data
Names: Meinking, Mary, author.
Title: Natural disasters / by Mary Meinking.
Description: Minneapolis, Minnesota : Pop!, 2019. | Series: Weather watch | Includes online resources and index.
Identifiers: ISBN 9781532160547 (lib.bdg.) | ISBN 9781532161667 (ebook) |
Subjects: LCSH: Natural disasters--Juvenile literature. | Weather--Juvenile literature. | Meteorology--juvenile literature.
Classification: DDC 551.5--dc23

Hello! My name is
Cody Koala

Pop open this book and you'll find QR codes like this one, loaded with information, so you can learn even more!

Scan this code* and others like it while you read, or visit the website below to make this book pop.

popbooksonline.com/natural-disasters

*Scanning QR codes requires a web-enabled smart device with a QR code reader app and a camera.

Table of Contents

Natural Disasters

Weather can quickly turn unsafe. It can become too hot, too cold, too wet, too dry, or too windy. Unsafe weather causes natural disasters.

Watch a video here!

Many Types

Hurricanes form over ocean water and slow down when they hit land. Their strong winds and heavy rain harm people and buildings.

For many years, hurricanes have been named after people.

Learn more here!

Tornadoes are cones of spinning wind that reach from storm clouds to the ground. Their strong winds destroy everything in their path.

In **blizzards**, strong winds blow loose snow around. It gets very cold. People and animals can get lost in the storm and die from the cold.

Chapter 3

Aftermath

Flooding can happen after heavy rains or hurricanes. Streets and homes fill with rising water. More people are affected by floods than by any other natural disaster.

Learn more here!

Too much water can also cause **landslides**. Water washes away the side of a mountain or hill. Homes slide along with it and are destroyed.

Too little water is also unsafe. Plants become as dry as paper and can catch on fire. **Wildfires** are hard to control and can be spread by the wind.

It can take firefighters weeks to control some wildfires.

Chapter 4

Be Prepared

People study the weather to guess when and where natural disasters might happen. This way everyone knows what to expect and how to prepare.

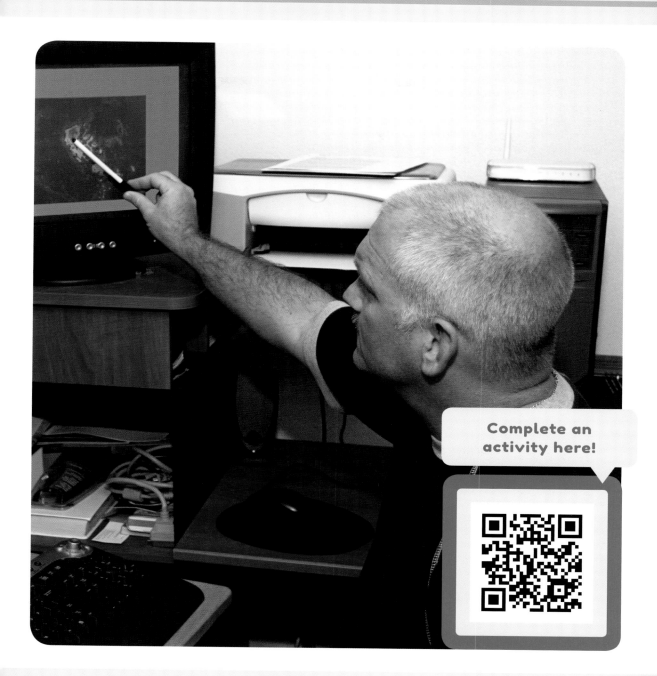

Complete an activity here!

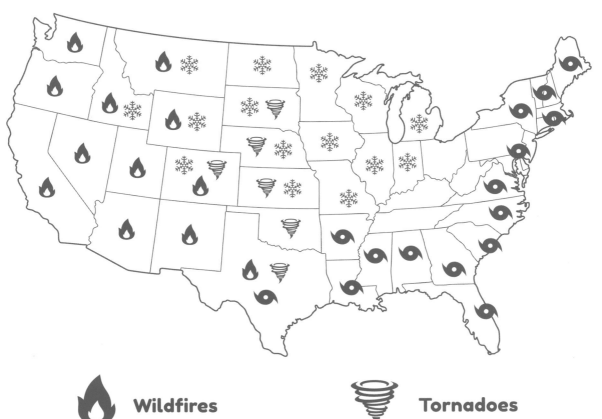

 Wildfires

 Tornadoes

 Blizzards

 Hurricanes

Some areas are more likely to see certain kinds of disasters. People can still be ready for natural disasters even if they happen with little notice.

Making Connections

Text-to-Self

Have you ever been in a natural disaster? What is the worst weather you've ever been in?

Text-to-Text

Have you read other books about the weather? What can you learn from books about the weather?

Text-to-World

Natural disasters happen around the world. How do they affect people?

Glossary

blizzard – a snowstorm with strong winds and cold temperatures that goes on for a long time.

hurricane – a large, powerful storm that forms over the ocean.

landslide – the sliding down of rock or earth from a mountain or hill.

tornado – a violent storm whose winds spin around on land.

wildfire – a large fire that grows quickly because of very dry plants and trees.

Index

Online Resources

popbooksonline.com

Thanks for reading this Cody Koala book!

Scan this code* and others like it in this book, or visit the website below to make this book pop!

popbooksonline.com/natural-disasters

*Scanning QR codes requires a web-enabled smart device with a QR code reader app and a camera.